Beyond The Headlines

Beyond The Headlines

My Perspective on the Robert Fisher Case

Jyquan Stewart

INGRAM SPARK

CONTENTS

1

Introduction

My name is Jy'Quan Stewart, and I have chosen to write the book "Beyond The Headlines" to express my perspective on the forthcoming landmark murder trial of Robert Fisher, scheduled at Rensselaer County Court on July 31, 2024. As the brother of the victim, Josefina Catherine Cunningham, who was murdered at 1552 Broadway in Rensselaer, New York, by Robert Fisher, I have been striving to bring national news attention to this case for a year by reaching out to major news outlets. The trial has finally arrived, and it's no ordinary proceeding; it's set to become a landmark event in the history of the United States of America.

2

Background Information on the case

A week before my three-year-old sister Josefina Catherine Cunningham was murdered, our mother encountered a man named Robert Fisher. On the day they met, she fell in love with him. I recall the time I met him; I was residing at 399 5th Ave in Troy, New York. It was around my birthday weekend, and I had gone to visit my mother while Josie was with her babysitter, Takyra. At my mother's house, located at 1552 Broadway in Rensselaer, New York, I encountered a white man wearing glasses. Initially, my mother mentioned he was the plumber, but as I sat there, she introduced him as her new boyfriend, Rob.

Then my mother mentioned that he would be joining us for dinner, so we went to a Hibachi restaurant. My mother ordered a Lyft on her phone, and we headed to the Hibachi Restaurant in Albany, New York. Robert tried to persuade me to drink liquor, and my mother attempted to have Robert Fisher add her credit card to his phone, but he refused. While eating, he talked about his friend "Dougie" who had a coyote and was Amish, mentioning that Dougie was expelled from his community. Robert also shared that he was raised in Guilderland, New York, and he received a portion of his mother's life insurance money, over $400,000, and described his family as country folk. After our meal, my mother called a Lyft, and we returned to her apartment in Rensselaer, New York. My mother and Robert spent the evening drinking a bottle of Bacardi and smoking marijuana. I went back to my apartment in Troy, New York.

A few days later, I called my mother and found out that she, along with my sister Josefina, were at Walmart shopping for groceries. I asked if I could speak with Josie, as she often chats with me on the phone. My mother informed me that Josie was browsing the children's toys section and would be taken back to her babysitter in Troy once they were finished.

On the Fourth of July, I took a bus to my mother's house to find out their plans for the holiday. They informed me that they were heading to the plaza to watch the fireworks and meet up with Robert's friend, Dougie. At the time, Josie was still at her babysitter's place. Later, my mother's friend Betty joined us, and we took a Lyft to the New York State Museum in Albany. As we exited the Lyft, Dougie called Robert to coordinate their meeting, but I learned that Dougie was involved in drug-related activities. Uncomfortable with the situation, I decided to leave and take the bus back to my apartment, wanting no part in it.

Three days later I realized I left my keys at my mother's house and After work I decided to take a Lyft to my mother's house. I remember seeing my sister Josefina she was alive as evermore and I remember heading to my mother's bathroom to use I saw Robert Fisher's drugs on our kitchen counter I was curious to know what it was. After I came back from the bathroom, I noticed Fisher eyes were blood red. I left them at my mother's home. That's the last time I saw Josefina.

Tragically, Josefina was left alone in the house with Fisher, and upon returning from Walmart, their mother found Josefina sound asleep. Tragically, Josefina was left alone in the house with Fisher, and upon returning from Walmart, our mother found Josefina sound asleep. In the middle of the night, our mother discovered Fisher deleting items from his phone while lying naked on the couch. She covered him with a towel, not knowing the horrors that had transpired. The following morning on July 7, 2024 Josefina's mother discovered her lifeless body, covered in bleach and with blue spots all over her and she called 911 while riding the bus to work, I received a call from my aunt, who told me that "Josie died." I immediately called an Uber to go to my mother's house. When I arrived, I saw yellow tape and my cousin, who was bent over in grief at the side of the house. I asked my mother where her boyfriend, Robert Fisher, was and she told me that the police had taken him to the station for questioning. She said that they had to throw him on the ground because he was trying to interfere with the investigation.

I then got into my aunt's car with my cousin and his father and we went to Albany Medical Center in Albany, New York, where Josie was pronounced dead. The hospital is where I first met Det. Sgt. Michael Deso of the Rensselaer Police Department, who would come to provide much-appreciated support to my family. There were three New York State detectives at Albany Medical Center.

My mother and I then got a ride from Capt. Robert Appleton of New York State Police to their headquarters for questioning on what happened the night before of Josefina's death. As investigations unfolded, it became apparent that Josefina had been brutally raped and murdered. The crime scene revealed blood on the bed, indicating a violent struggle.

Robert Fisher has entered a not-guilty plea in the Rensselaer County City Court on August 2, 2023. Everyone has been waiting for the trial for a year now. The trial has officially been set for July 31, 2024.

3

Personal Experience and Thoughts

As I sit here, trying to process the devastating loss of my little sister Josefina Catherine Cunningham, I'm met with a mix of emotions - grief, anger, sadness, and frustration. The news of her tragic death at the hands of Robert Fisher has left our family reeling, and the upcoming trial feels like a crucial step towards seeking justice for her memory.

As I look back on the memories we shared, I'm reminded of the tiny hand that held mine, the giggles we shared over silly jokes, and the way she would snuggle up close to me during bedtime stories. Josefina was more than just a child - she was a bright light in our lives, a reminder of the beauty and innocence of childhood.

But as I reflect on her life, I'm also confronted with the harsh reality of the world we live in. A world where children are vulnerable to violence and exploitation. A world where even the smallest and most innocent can be taken from us too soon. The trial is not just about seeking justice for Josefina; it's about acknowledging the systemic failures that allowed this tragedy to occur. It's about recognizing that our society has failed to protect its most vulnerable members, and that we must do better.

As I think about Josefina's dream of becoming a firefighter, I'm reminded of her determination and courage. She may have been taken from us too soon, but her spirit will live on through our efforts to make sure that no other child suffers a similar fate.

I hope that this trial will be a turning point in our community's collective consciousness. I hope that it will spark a national conversation about child protection and the importance of holding perpetrators accountable for their actions. I hope that it will inspire us to work together to create a safer, more just world for all children.

As I look ahead to the trial, I know that it won't be easy. I know that there will be difficult days ahead, but I also know that justice is within reach. And as I stand alongside my family and the community, I'm reminded that we are not alone in this fight.

We are Josefina's advocates, and we will not rest until justice is served. We will not rest until every child is protected and every perpetrator is held accountable with the Death Penalty

We will not rest until we have created a world where innocence is cherished and protected.

For Josefina's memory, we will fight. We will fight for justice, for compassion, and for a world where every child can grow up free from fear and harm.

4

Analysis and Opinion of the case

Rensselaer County Public Defender Arthur Frost has taken on the challenging task of representing Robert J. Fisher, the defendant in the highly publicized trial for the rape and murder of 3-year-old Josefina C. Cunningham. Fisher, who pleaded not guilty to the charges, faces a trial scheduled to begin on July 31 at the Rensselaer County Court.

Frost's decision to defend Fisher has drawn attention and controversy. The public is wondering why Arthur Frost is defending a child rapist and murderer. However, Frost is determined to ensure that Fisher receives a fair trial and is not guilty until proven otherwise. He will meticulously examine the voluminous discovery in this case, including the DNA evidence linking Fisher to the child. He will explore any potential flaws or inconsistencies in the evidence and address the allegation that Fisher attempted to interfere with the investigation.

Frost will argue that Fisher's actions were unrelated to guilt and were merely a reaction to the intense scrutiny. He acknowledges Fisher's extensive criminal record but will emphasize that past convictions do not automatically prove guilt in this specific case. Each case must be evaluated independently, and Frost will present Fisher's background, struggles, and personal circumstances to humanize him in the eyes of the jury. This approach aims to foster empathy and challenge preconceptions.

Frost will also explore alternative scenarios that could explain the evidence, raising questions about other potential suspects or circumstances. He may use expert witnesses to provide testimony on various aspects of the case, such as forensic science or psychological profiling.

The debate centers around whether Josefina's murder should be classified as a hate crime. Advocates argue that the crime was motivated by prejudice against her race, given that Josefina was an African American child. They point to the brutality of the act and the innocence of the victim as evidence that this was more than a random act of violence. The racial dynamics in the case have raised questions about systemic racism and bias within the criminal justice system.

The use of artificial intelligence (AI) is becoming increasingly prevalent in legal cases, including this one. AI can be used to analyze vast amounts of data and identify key trends and patterns in the case, allowing for more effective investigation and prosecution strategies.

"We are using AI to analyze vast amounts of data and identify key trends and patterns in the case," said one of the AI experts working on the case. "This allows us to target our outreach efforts and ensure that we are reaching the right people with the right message." AI can help amplify our voices and reach people who might not otherwise have heard about the case.

The lack of communication and progress in this case has been frustrating for many involved, including Josefina's family members. In a news article, one family member expressed their frustration and suggested that perhaps Donald J. Trump should handle the case. However, it is essential to remember that justice should be served based on facts, evidence, and law, not political affiliations or personal opinions.

The Rensselaer County District Attorney's Office should continue to work diligently to ensure that justice is served in this case.

As the trial approaches, it is crucial that all parties involved remain focused on finding truth and justice for Josefina C. Cunningham and her family. The use of AI can help facilitate this process by providing valuable insights and assistance throughout the investigation.

In conclusion, Arthur Frost's decision to defend Robert J. Fisher has sparked controversy, but he remains committed to ensuring a fair trial for his client. The use of AI in this case highlights the importance of technology in modern legal proceedings. As we move forward with this trial, it is essential that we prioritize justice, fairness, and compassion for all parties involved.

The trial of Robert J. Fisher is not just about finding justice for Josefina C. Cunningham; it is about ensuring that our criminal justice system is fair, equitable, and just for all individuals involved. It is about recognizing systemic racism and bias within our society and working towards creating a more just society for everyone.

As we navigate this complex and emotionally charged case, it is essential that we remain focused on finding truth and serving justice for all parties involved.

5

Conclusion and Final Thoughts

his case is not just another trial; it is poised to go down in our nation's history, and it's expected to cause worldwide outrage. The gravity of the situation is evident, and it's crucial that the Rensselaer County Court takes immediate action to ensure the safety and security of all involved. The potential for large crowds and protests necessitates a comprehensive plan to manage the situation, including the closure of roads surrounding the courthouse and providing police escorts for the family of the victim and key witnesses.

The concerns about the court's ability to handle the trial are valid, given the high-profile nature of the case and the potential for public outcry. It's essential that the court recognizes the gravity of this case and takes steps to prepare appropriately to ensure the trial proceeds in a safe and orderly manner. The world is watching, and the Rensselaer County Court must rise to the occasion. The court's response to this trial will not only impact the local community but will also be a reflection of our nation's commitment to justice.

This horrific act has left an indelible mark on our family, prompting them to question the adequacy of the current legal system in New York State. The family believes that there are sick people who sex offenders are and that New York State is not doing enough to address this issue. They plan to expose New York State's unrestricted and perverted laws with the National Press, believing that the United States needs to see what's going on.

In 2007, New York State abolished the death penalty, citing concerns about its cruelty. However, the family is now urging society to reconsider what constitutes true cruelty - the calculated murder of innocent children or holding those responsible accountable through capital punishment. According to the U.S. Department of Justice, there were 1,476 child homicides across America in 2019 alone. Each case represents a life cut short and a family forever scarred by loss.

The case has gripped the state and beyond, drawing parallels with the historic case of Emmett Till, which sparked nationwide outrage and became a catalyst for the civil rights movement. Like the Till case, this trial has the potential to leave a lasting impact on our society and our justice system. Given the gravity of the case and the public interest it has generated, it is anticipated that there will be over 1,000 people in the courtroom. This unprecedented number of attendees underscores the importance of this case to the community and the state at large.

The horrifying details of the crime scene, including Josefina's lifeless body covered in bleach and blue spots, have sent shockwaves through the community. This case has garnered significant attention in New York State. Our family is determined to bring these details to international light, hoping to raise awareness about child abuse and murder and push for change in our justice system.

It is essential that we acknowledge that this case is not just about Josefina or her family; it's about every child who has been victimized by abuse or murder. It's about every family who has been left shattered by loss. It's about every community that has been affected by violence and trauma. This case has brought attention to an issue that needs to be addressed - an issue that affects us all.

As we move forward with this trial, it's crucial that we prioritize justice and accountability. We must ensure that those responsible for crimes like these are held accountable for their actions. We must also work towards creating a society where children are protected from harm and abuse.The Rensselaer County Court must take immediate action to address these concerns and provide a safe and secure environment for all involved in this trial. The world is watching, and it's imperative that we rise to this occasion. this case has the potential to be a turning point in our national conversation about the Death Penalty for those who commit such crimes.

www.ingramcontent.com/pod-product-compliance
Lightning Source LLC
LaVergne TN
LVHW022327200926
848481LV00004B/1451
* 9 7 9 8 3 3 0 2 4 1 3 1 6 *